A little boy who had a little fling

Words by Norman C. Habel
Pictures by Jim Roberts

A PURPLE PUZZLE TREE BOOK

COPYRIGHT © 1972
CONCORDIA PUBLISHING HOUSE,
ST. LOUIS, MISSOURI
CONCORDIA PUBLISHING HOUSE LTD.,
LONDON, E. C. 1
MANUFACTURED IN THE
UNITED STATES OF AMERICA
ISBN 0-570-06517-8

There was a little biddle boy
Who had a little fiddle harp
And he played and serenaded Saul the king.
He had some fun a-fighting lions
And a hairy scarey bear.
Oh, the kiddle always did his little thing.

And so that little biddle boy
Who had a little fiddle harp
Joined the people of the puzzle that we sing.
Because our God once picked that boy
Who had such sassy rascal ways
To be His spangle, dangle, high and mighty king.

And this is how that little boy
with his little harp
came to be a king
with a very big heart:

One day the long-legged Philistines
came out to fight King Saul
and his shaky, shivering soldiers.
Then this giant guy Goliath
came booming down the field:
BLUMP BOOM,
BLUMP BOOM, BOOOOO.

Yes, Goliath was a giant
over nine feet tall.
His coat was bronze
and his armor was bronze,
his pants were bronze
and his helmet was bronze,
and he looked like a big bronze wall.

He thundered down the field:
BLUMP BOOM,
BLUMP BOOM, BOOOOO.
"Does anyone want to fight with me
before we murder you?"

No one wanted to fight the giant.
Would you?

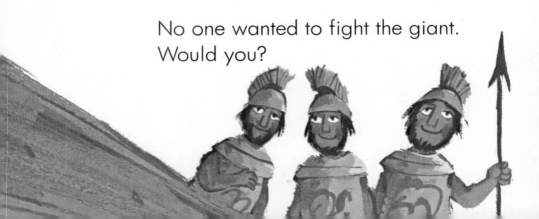

There was a little biddle boy
Who had a little diddle toy
For the kiddle always did his little thing.
He was a kiddle without armor
And a shepherd without spear
But he'd whistle with his silly little sling.

Now that little boy, called David,
went out to meet Goliath,
who laughed his heavy head off
when he saw that silly kid:
"You silly little kid
with your funny little sling,
will you beat me like a dog?
Shall I dance for you
and bark for you
like a little puppy dog?"

"My God is not a Jack-in-the-box,"
said that sassy rascal David,
"but Lord of all this land.
He can kill a goofy giant
with nothing in His hand."

Then David picked a polished pebble,
bright and round and smooth.
He slipped it quickly in his sling
and swung it round his head.

THOOP!
The stone shot through the air,
whistling like a train:
SSSS SSSS SSSS THOOP!
It hit the giant on the head
and dug into his brain.

David grabbed the giant's sword
to chop his huge head off
as all the laughing Philistines
cursed the kid and ran.

Well, that little boy, called David,
soon became a hero,
and old king Saul was jealous
when the people sang this song:

There was a little biddle boy
Who had a little biddle fling
And his heart was billy brave and really tall.

He had some fun a-fighting lions
And a giant big and mean
And he whistled while he won more fights
than Saul.

Saul became so jealous
his heart was filled with rage.
So David played his harp
to soothe the old king's nerves.
But that only made things worse,
until the king picked up his spear
and flung it right at David.

Then the chase began
as Saul kept hunting David—
over slippery mountains,
across the sizzling sand,
and into slimy caves
up and down the land.

So David fled to Gath,
where Achish was the king,
a very filthy Philistine
who was ready for anything.
When he saw young David,
he said, "Well, look who's here!
Isn't this the crazy kid
who killed Goliath last year?"

When David saw they knew him,
he started to slobber and spit.
He clawed and scratched and bellowed
and rolled his eyes in pain,
so everybody thought
the crazy kid had gone insane.

Well, Achish didn't want a "kook" around
to bring him more bad luck.
So he told the lad to "run off home
and never ever come back."

After that little fling with the Philistines
David lived with his friends in the caves,
and Saul kept trying to catch him
day after day after day.

One day King Saul came by
the cave where David was hiding,
and stepped inside for a minute,
just to go to the toilet.

David, the dirty rascal,
crept up behind the king.
He grabbed the long, red robe
that Saul left on the ground.
He cut it in half
with a swish of his sword
and whisked it away
without saying a word.

All the king's horses
and all the king's men
giggled like a bunch of kids
when they saw King Saul
with his mighty mini-skirt.

When Saul reached the next hill,
David came out of the cave.
He waved the end of the king's robe
high at the point of a stick,
and everyone shouted, Wooopeee!

But David said, "Saul,
you are God's king for our people.
I didn't kill you today
when you were helpless
back in that dark, wet cave.
So let us make peace
and work together again."

But Saul didn't listen.
And when the Philistines came again,
David, the hero, was missing.
So Saul and three of his sons
were killed in that filthy war,
and David was very sad.
For Saul was God's first king
in His purple puzzle plan.

Oh yes, there was a little boy
Who had a little fiddle fling
And his heart was billy brave and flying free.
That's why this little biddle boy
Grew up to be a mighty king
In God's churple, purple, people, puzzle tree.

OTHER TITLES

the PURPLE PUZZLE TREE